SEBASTIAN CUR[...]

GLOW

for Solo Piano

T0055887

BOOSEY & HAWKES

DISTRIBUTED BY

HAL•LEONARD®

7777 W. BLUEMOUND RD. P.O. BOX 13819 MILWAUKEE, WI 53213

www.boosey.com
www.halleonard.com

Commissioned by Wigmore Hall, with the support of André Hoffmann,
President of the Fondation Hoffmann, a Swiss grant-making foundation.
The commission has been made possible by a financial contribution from the
Composition Commission Fund of The Royal Concertgebouw.
The Composition Commission Fund is set up by a private donor with the intention of
stimulating the development of new music and reaching a larger audience. The fund is
managed by Het Concertgebouw Fonds.
Co-commissioned by the Aspen Music Festival and School, Robert Spano, Music Director.

COMPOSER NOTE

When pianist Inon Barnatan asked me to write him a new work, he had a particular stipulation: that I somehow connect my piece with Ravel's *Gaspard de la Nuit,* which he would program alongside my new work. This seemed an intriguing proposition. I decided not to refer to any musical material in Gaspard, but took my cue from the textual elements that accompany the score. The title of the work comes from a collection of poems by Aloysius Bertrand. It is generally translated as "The Treasurer (or Jewel Keeper) of the Night."

I imagined jewels gleaming from some narrow light source in the otherwise enshrouding darkness. This was my starting point: light at night. Indeed the poems that Ravel selects from Bertrand's collection refer to light within the general context of darkness: "windows lit by the gloomy rays of the moon," or "the moon glitters in the sky like a silver shield...." In creating my piece, *Glow,* I imagined all the myriad ways objects are lit at night and settled on seven: moonlight (a nod to Ravel), a simple spark momentarily illuminating darkness, a lighthouse in the distance, the metric flashing of a strobe light in a nightclub, the colorful exuberance of fireworks exploding above, a spiral galaxy slowly rotating in distant space, and the embers of a fire as it fades.

The basis for *Glow,* then, was a simple synesthesia where light = sound and dark = silence. One can continue the analogue with brightness = volume and color = pitch, though it's really only the first that was essential to me. In *strobe light* short, clipped fragments of sound are bounded by rests, giving the impression that something is missing, gaps that cannot be perceived. In *lighthouse* a resonant figure is repeated with dark spaces of silence in between. It repeats relentlessly except that it grows and subsides in intensity, as if one were to move closer to or further from the light source. In including *fireworks,* I could not but in some way call to mind another piece: that of Debussy's famed prelude by the same name. My rendering of fireworks are far more literal that Debussy's. Between each firework display, with its own colors and form, there are pauses. It is only at the end that a continuous and chaotic series of launches lights the sky cacophonously. In the last movement, *embers,* disembodied fragments from other movements glimmer briefly before fading into the dark.

In referring to the last movement of *Gaspard*, Ravel said "I wanted to make a caricature of romanticism. Perhaps it got the better of me." I guess one could say that *Glow* is a synesthetic, ironic, caricature of Impressionist piano music......but I keep my distance.......or do I?

TABLE OF CONTENTS

GLOW

1. Moonlight

SEBASTIAN CURRIER
(2013)

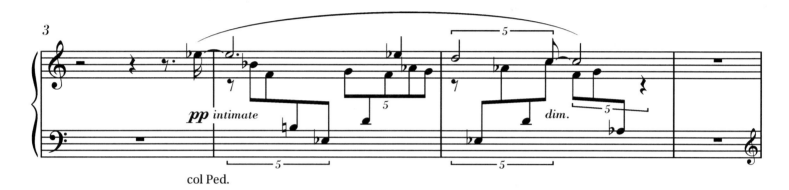

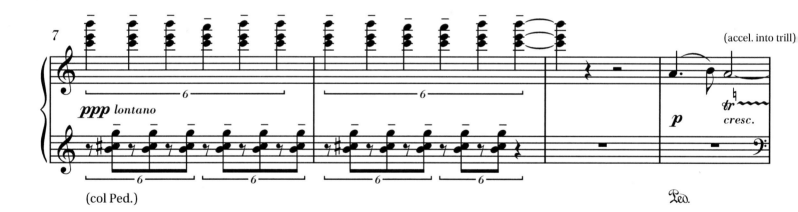

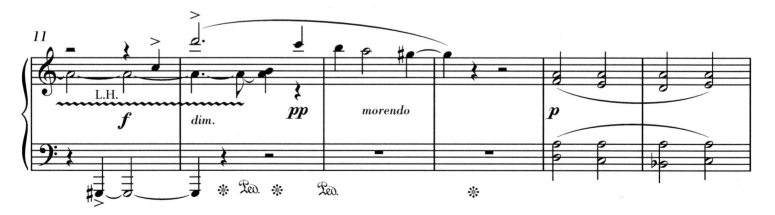

979-0-051-09821-7

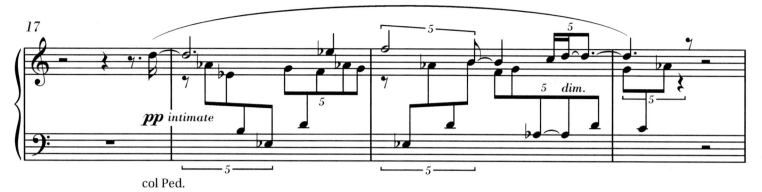

2. Spark

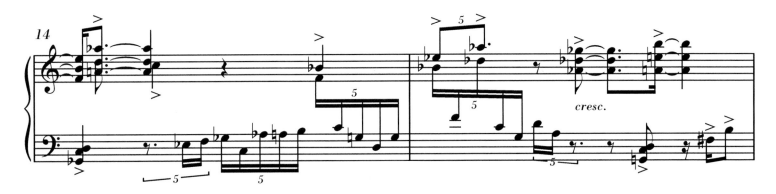

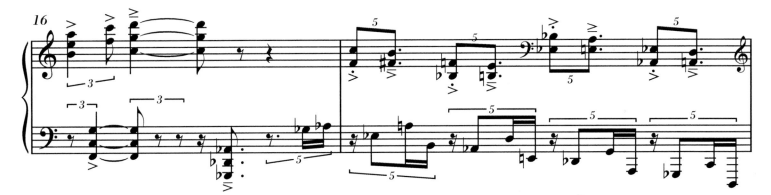

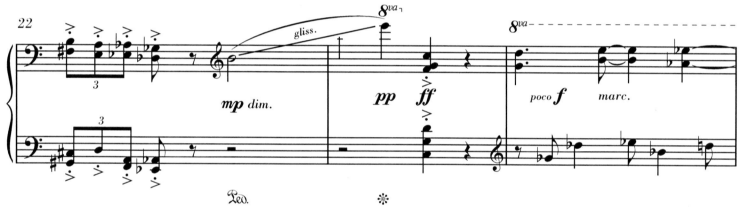

3. Lighthouse

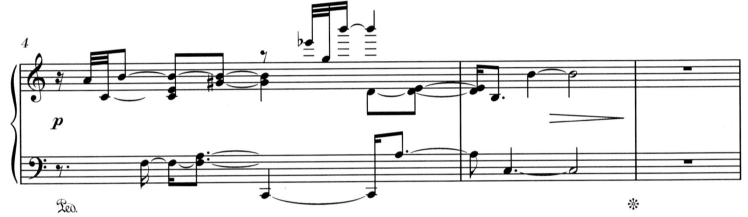

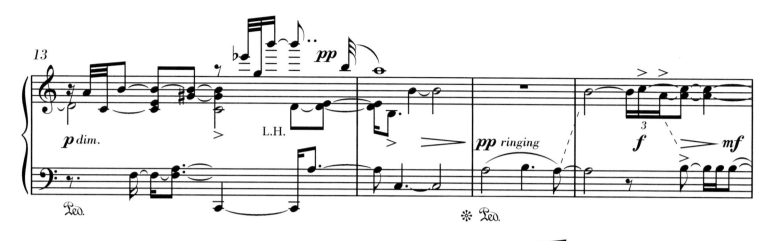

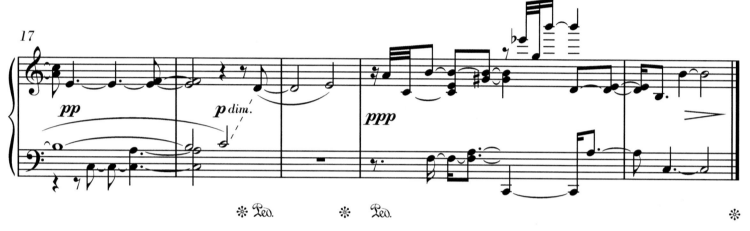

4. Strobe Light

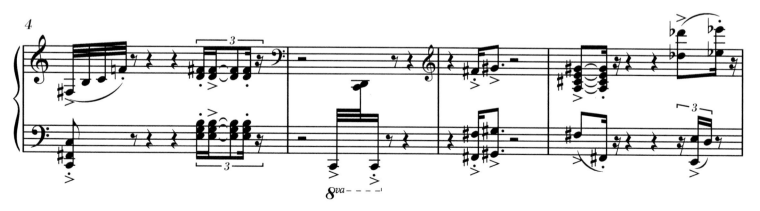

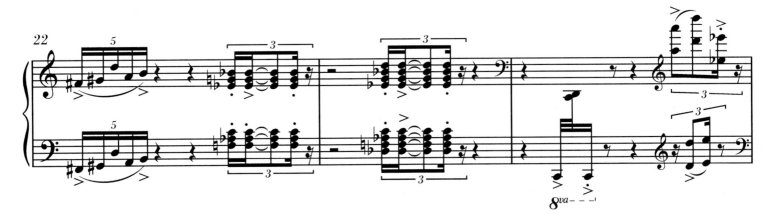

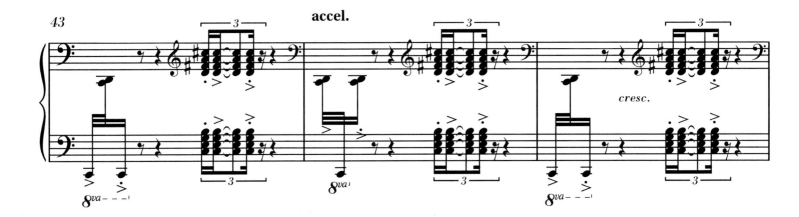

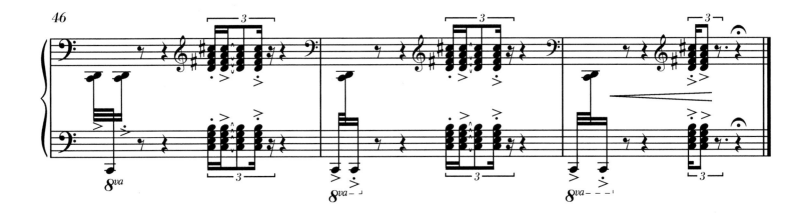

5. Fireworks

♩ = c. 138

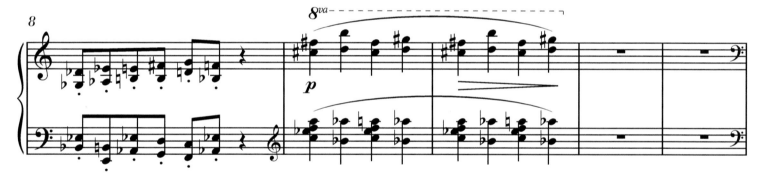

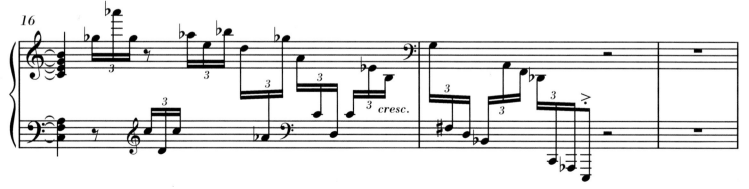

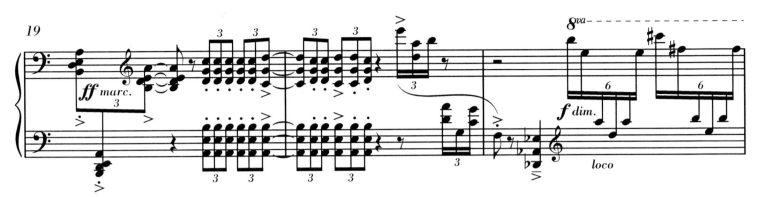

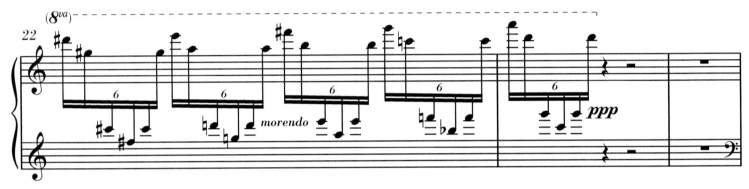

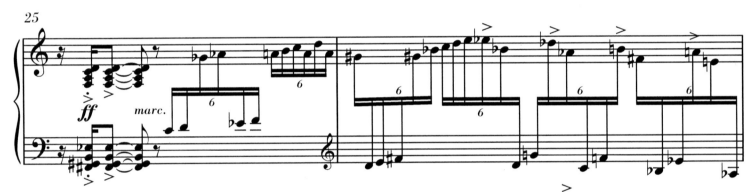

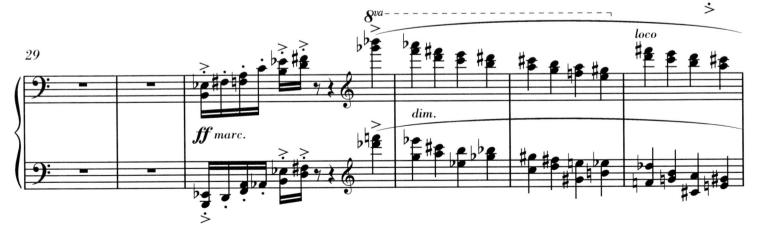

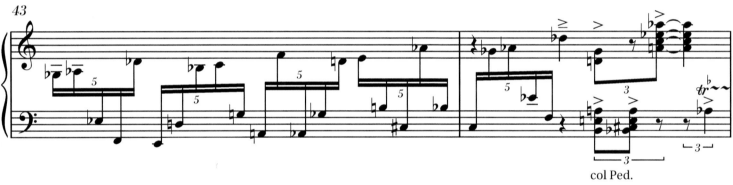

col Ped.

col Ped.

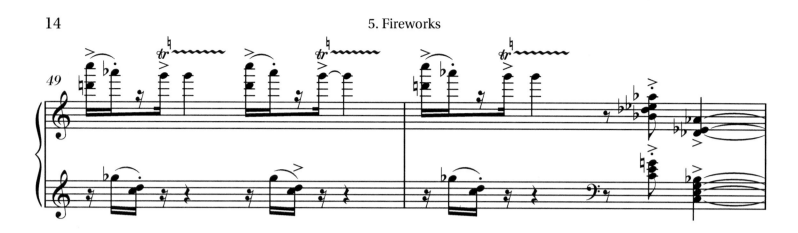

col Ped.

(col Ped.) gradually use increasing amount of sustain pedal

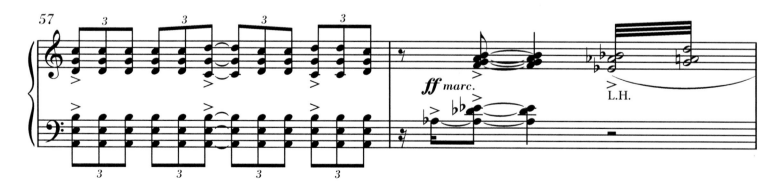

V.S.

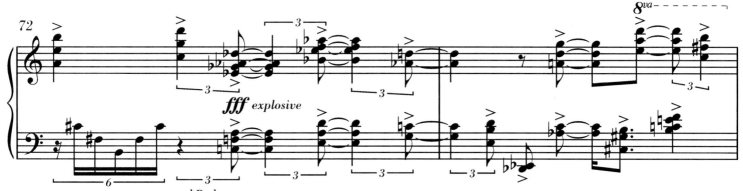

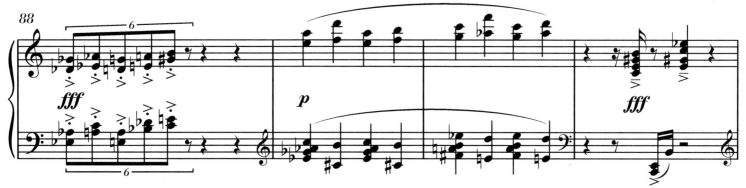

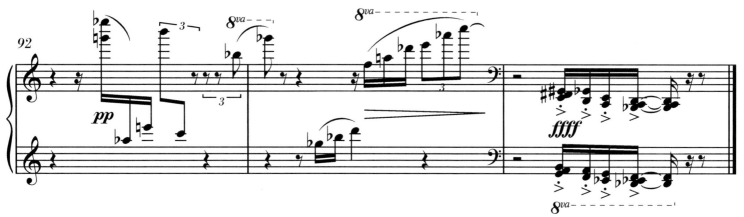

6. Spiral Galaxy

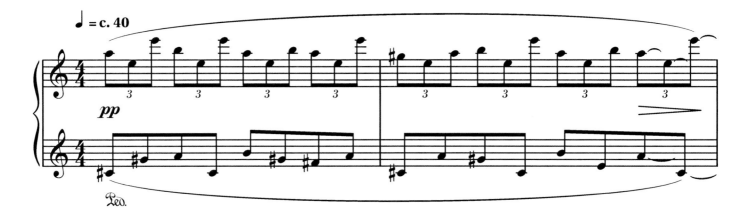

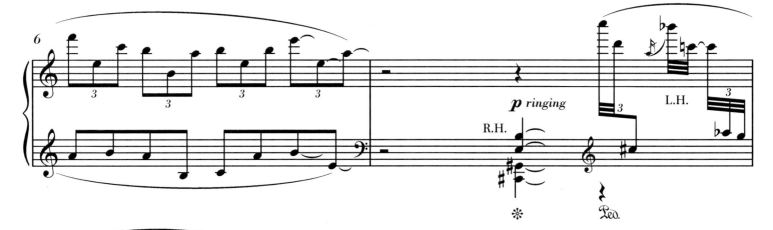

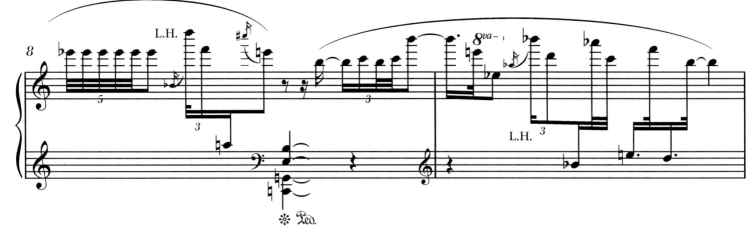

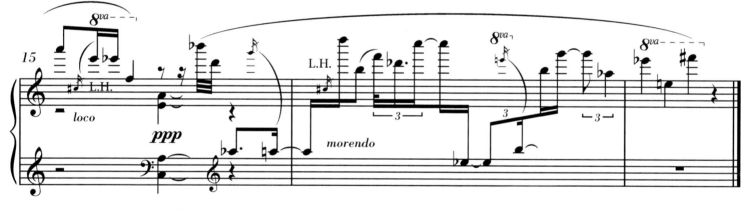

7. Embers

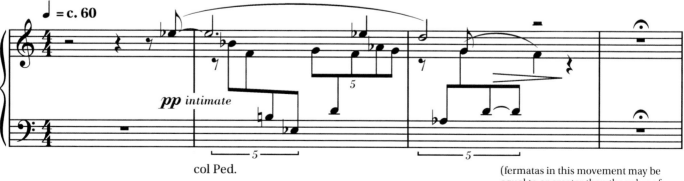

(fermatas in this movement may be
equal to or greater than the value of
the rests, at the performer's discretion)

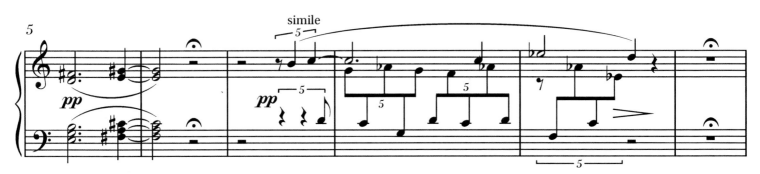

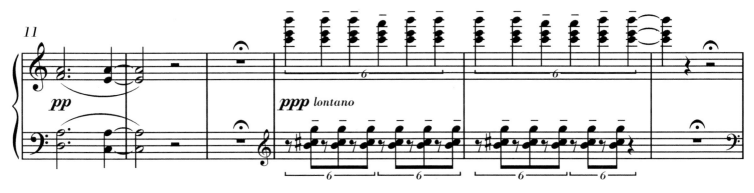

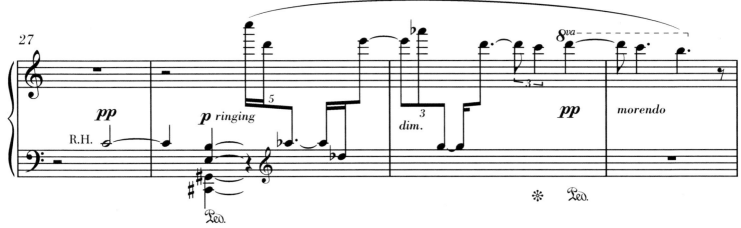

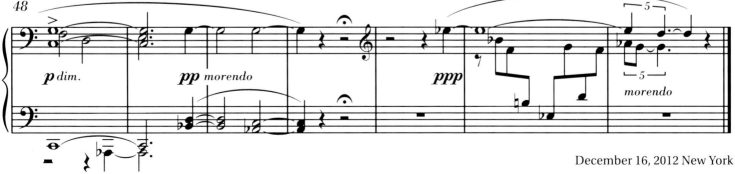

December 16, 2012 New York